A Festivity of Love

A Festivity of Love

Poems, Verse, and Prose from St Endellion

Compiled by

Judith Pollinger and

Paul S. Fiddes

Firedint Publishing Oxford

Firedint Publishing Oxford
76 Kingston Road
Oxford OX2 6RJ

ISBN 978-1-9999407-3-7

September 2019

Preface

In the Ancient World, four aspects of love were often identified: affection (*storge*), friendship (*philia*), passion (*eros*) and charity or self-giving (*agape*). For those who thought about the matter carefully, it seemed that these were not four types of love, but dimensions of one love, and this is confirmed in the poems, verse and prose that make up this small book. They cross the boundaries, not only in expressions of love for life-partners and for God, but also in the cases of love for Cornwall and for cats! It is because love cannot be categorized that we have chosen to organize these pieces, except for the first which sets the scene in North Cornwall, simply alphabetically by writer.

Here are poems dense with ambiguity, poignant prose, and light verse designed to raise a smile. Like love itself, this collection is inclusive, containing poems by published and prize-winning poets, and pieces by amateur poets and versifiers. Here are celebrations of faithful love, elegies of lost love, and affirmations of the enduring nature of love in the face of the passing of time and the horizon of death. In the words of St Paul's Hymn to Love, "Now remain faith, hope and love, these three; but the greatest of these is love."

It is appropriate to quote St Paul, as this collection was made as a resource for a special service at the Collegiate Church of St Endellion, North Cornwall in October 2019, marking the Seventh North Cornwall Book Festival. The theme of the Festival was love, reflected in the title of this book, "A Festivity of Love". All the writers are not from North Cornwall, but all have a connection in some way with St Endellion Church, or with Endelienta, a charitable organization for music, literature, arts and spirituality associated with the

Church. A number are members of the St Endellion Poetry Group.

Three of the poems, by Jane Draycott, Helen Jagger, and Christopher Southgate, were written for a liturgy called "Living by the Risks of Love", based on Shakespeare's play *The Merchant of Venice*, and first presented by the North Cornwall Cluster of Churches at St Minver Church in November 2018. The poems portray the experience of love of three women in the the play—Portia, Jessica and Nerissa—and as with all the pieces in the book, readers will recognize themselves in them.

Christiana Richardson

Christiana Richardson lives in Redruth. She loves to explore the world through poetry and has enjoyed performing her poems in "The Writers' Block Speakeasy" events in Pool, Cornwall.

Why I love North Cornwall

Trees grown bent
in the direction of the winds
Cliff top paths daring
with jagged rocks below
Glistening stones on grainy sands
rattle in the tide
White horses race
over tops of towering waves
Early morning dips
whatever time of year
Mizzle, rain and storms
freshen smog-free air
Old-time jukeboxes
playing in the corner
of public houses full
with music, songs and banter
Fresh pepp'ry pasties
made by aunt's skilled hand
With tender gristle-free steak
From her village butcher's shop
Happy travellers arriving
dipping in cold pools
Intrigued, suncreamed children
searching for adventure

A FESTIVAL OF LOVE

Methodist chapels' congregation
welcoming with smiles
Traditional markets in old towns
And thick clotted cream

Louise Ansdell

Louise Ansdell lives in Oxford. She is a barrister, a Jane Austen devotee, an incipient empty-nester and a bookworm

Devotion

When I survey the wondrous cat
Who on the sunny landing lies,
My greatest trial I count but naught,
And pour my love on this feline prize.

Forgive me, Lord, that I should boast
About a cat I find divine.
Apollo, he immortal is –
The captain of this heart of mine.

Jane Draycott

Jane Draycott Draycott teaches English and Creative Writing at the University of Lancaster. Her collection ***Over*** *(Carcanet) was shortlisted for the 2009 T S Eliot Prize. Nominated three times for the Forward Prize for Poetry, her first two full collections,* ***Prince Rupert's Drop*** *and* ***The Night Tree*** *(Carcanet/Oxford Poets), were both Poetry Book Society Recommendations.*

Nerissa: The Landing Stage

From "Living by the Risks of Love", a liturgy based on Shakespeare's *The Merchant of Venice*

The wind's unsettled round the jetty,
steps up ashore with us among our skirts.
So much that isn't clear remains suspended
here – our green place, home – like particles
of darkness in the daytime atmosphere.

The clearest thing in sight's this water,
its restless glass like weather in the palm,
our own anatomy, invisible and indivisible,
like nothing in the hand but in the ring
of the lagoon as solid as a leaded door.

With every crossing something comes
and goes in us, some hidden cargo
that we trust out on the headstrong channel
even when the moonstruck tide runs set
against the wind like a determined girl.

What's in a ring? In the dim-lit streets
the future's masked, the past's adrift

in mist. There's no experiment
to estimate the all we've hazarded:
we take the risk, welcome the mystery.

It may be that heaven's mosaic floor
is just a deck, no more, with us held
in the hold, the stars small chinks
of daylight through the boards –
not gold but silver, which we settle for.

We stand here at the landing stage
in plainest sight to meet our husbands.
Who in the fast-returning morning
will be my torchbearer, to see
what's hiding in this restless light?

Paul S. Fiddes

Paul S. Fiddes is an Ecumenical Prebendary of St Endellion Collegiate Church and Professor of Systematic Theology in the University of Oxford, specializing in the relationship between theology and creative literature.

Three for Marion

On her 35th birthday

If you feel part of the scenery, unremarked,
merely familiar like a well-worn jacket,
"Mother of two", with no time for Keynes or Barth,
aim-lost, as a returned-to-sender packet:
think this. Each the other's self in comfort wearing
means heart's ease promised to those yoke-bearing.
We find each other new in our sons' faces
and hear our love on instruments new-strung,
your keen mind cuts a way in casual places
where many walk more sure, and I among.

(1981)

A FESTIVAL OF LOVE

On seeing a "unicorn horn" (or a narwhal tusk)
in a museum,

It stood against the wall, its tip abrupt –
cut short in quest of costly remedy
against the poisonous hate that could erupt,
pretending love while making threnody –
yet still an eight-foot call upon belief
that such a weight could crown a bearded throat,
be carried by a beast scarce larger than a goat,
laying love's burden down for love's relief.

Weavers of wool and words had felt that load,
catching no whiff of salt and northern seas,
ivory tusks buoyed up where currents flowed,
no maiden's lap required for lover's ease.
    For fifty years I've known where love has led:
    in your garden of delight I lay my head.

(2019)

A FESTIVAL OF LOVE

A Christmas card for Marion:
Adoration of the Magi by Pieter Bruegel

From a thousand winter landscapes I choose two:
One the sturdy burghers' neighbourhood of wide plains
And plainer sense, and one the hilly derring-do
Of Narnia, where beasts speak, and the Lion reigns.
Enter we each its stable, this a soundly-built device,
This fragile with patterns of courtesy and sacrifice.
Within them we adore the mystery of love,
Love in each other born anew, and from above.

David Foster

David Foster lives in Chichester and until two years ago lived in the parish of St Endellion. He was made a Lay Prebendary of the Collegiate Church of St Endellion. He is married to Sue and he rejoices that they have 'seven wonderful grandchildren'.

The Bench

The bandstand on the promenade was looking worse for wear; certainly a pale reflection of the days in its prime but still surrounded by the original wrought iron seats. They sat there every day on the same bench; an elderly couple arriving about two thirty and staying for an hour or so. Rain or shine, nothing but the severest winter weather caused them to alter their daily habits. Not much passed between them but occasionally she might say something or point to the beach.

Although I knew it was an intrusion I was eventually drawn to sit down and join them.

She spoke. "This is our bench you see. He doesn't talk since the stroke. My sister wants me to move closer but we can't leave our bench. This is our bench. Every Sunday afternoon when the band was here this was where we came to do our courting. This is our special place. We used to get here early because it had to be this bench. This is our bench you see, because we could watch the band but we could also get a lovely view of the beach. We used to so enjoy watching the goings-on with children playing their beach games and we would make such plans for our own family." She paused for a moment and looked out over the sands. “But it never happened; we weren’t blessed you see. Still we always had each other and that’s all that matters he would say. And we still have each other – don’t we?” His pale watery eyes stared at the deserted sands without expression but I noticed that when she said this he gently squeezed her hand.

My Christmas Love

How can I tell you all my affections,
The short days seem so long till you are here
For you are my queen of all confections,
No other could I ever hold so dear.
Your moist and luscious fragrance on my lips,
Who first conceived of that amazing plan,
Which other special moments will eclipse
To crush the almonds and to make a marzipan.
I cannot put in words quite how I feel:
Taste of mixed spices from a tropical isle,
Sultanas, raisins, currants and candied peel
With icing made like snow to bring a smile.
Will I wait a year before once more you come?
If so, I must relish every single crumb.

I'm not in love

I fell in love at seventeen
And twenty-one, plus times between
The same again at twenty-two
But always so hard to see it through.
This was it! Then to my surprise
There was another pair of bright eyes.
Surely this time it was the real thing
Perhaps even the moment to buy a ring.
Whoops, suddenly just as before
I found a new love at twenty-four.
Could there be something wrong with me;
Am I incapable of constancy?
I hoped this bond was made in heaven;
Well, it nearly lasted to twenty-seven!
Since then flames have brightly shone
Flickered out and soon were gone.
But now that I am thirty-four
Of one thing I'm completely sure:
Though it seems odd to thus proclaim
"I shall not fall in love again!"
There is no doubt that this is true
For all has changed since I met you.
To talk of love is quite absurd
When I hang upon your every word,
From first thing to midnight chime
My thoughts are with you all the time.
I worry about you while you sleep
That your dreams are sweet and your slumbers deep.
It's quite irrelevant what you wear,
How you look or style your hair.
The slightest thing that you require

Becomes my one and only desire.
And pray that whatever may betide
I'll be always by your side.
What I feel is something new
It can't be love, I'm sure that's true.
So with much joy I'll say it plain
"I'll never fall in love again!"

Suranjit Gain

Suranjit Gain lives in Bangladesh and was educated in both Bangladesh and India, receiving a congratulatory degree in literature. He describes himself simply as "a poet".

Love is life

Love is life;
without attachment we have no worth.
It is like nectar;
oh nice so sweet.
Affection is the best donation of god;
it's like the heaven.
Love is a little word;
but deeper than oceans.
Jesus Christ, the symbol of love;
great, memorable, a soaring dove.
Layli Majnu, the best lovers,
Obtain eternity in the earth.
We win the atlas with our love-affairs;
pray for the universe to be lovely.
Let us love each other;
oh my dear brother and sister.

My love

I am in love with you;
it's the real pride of mine.
Thou remainest in my heart;
I am for ever of thine.
What's thy expectation
unknown to me?
I expect thou;
my love is innocent.
My thoughts are not for an other,
only for you.
In every succeeding life
thou art new.

Jeff Hankins

Jeff Hankins lives in Deri, in the Darren Valley, in the former-mining area of South East Wales. He has spent most of his working life teaching English in secondary schools and tertiary colleges, as well as teaching in South America for some years with an Anglican Mission Society. Now retired, he continues to write poetry and songs which he performs when and where he can.

The Gentling of Polly

We've never got on, I know;
And even now I cannot stand
Your daytime skittishness –
The worrying of paper scraps, your claws
Carelessly hooking stitches from the sofa.
And I abhor your disdain for the outdoors,
Your ominous retreat to cupboard-tops,
Your bristling, arching, threatening to leap –
Nothing in that pantomime amuses me.

And yet, at night, when I'm the last one up,
Brainlessly inert before the made-for-TV movies,
You pad towards me, pawing at my chest,
Tentatively nuzzling me, trying me out; a purr
As loud as heaven, whether plea or tease or thrill
Left undisclosed, but how it deepens,
Breathing downwards to a broadening growl
Seeming contentment, as my slow hand
Travels your sinuousness, despite itself.
And here we stay – fallen into
Familiar smoothing rhythms –

A FESTIVAL OF LOVE

Tidal, the way – I suppose – that when we sleep
Dark waves reach up
To lap and lap and level the rippled sand,
stroking the shore.

Tomorrow when you scowl at me again
There may be one degree less iciness
Within your narrowed eyes.
Who knows, there might be
Slightly less of malice in
my customary kick – and as you dodge it,
A touch less venom in your own habitual hiss.

It is/ I am

Not then with an IT IS at the start
Fragmenting itself without sense,
Cold particles in faceless collision
Morphing randomly through vacuous space
To this, to all of this –
This smile, this rich connectedness,
The shiverings of light and nuances of irony,
Quick twinklings of mischief,
Empathy's bright shadowings
And colours, tastes and teases,
Puzzles, mysteries and all that we call craft
And consciousness, fumblings of awkward affection
And the subtle choreographies of passion,
Tumbles and trills of tune, the held breath
Of sudden birdsong...

And if all these could swim back, grateful,
Trace the source, would they find only
One small empty cave, one dry blank atom?
Personhood proving just so many mirage-tricks
Draining back to dust?

O, no, but with a glorious I AM it starts:
What brooded over void was one great will
With tenderhanded care,
Deliberateness of artistry,
By very nature giving –
Spilling out worlds of fingerprint and heartbeat
Whereby, from streams of meaning, we arrive

At this, this smile, this rich connectedness,
All validated in his life and breath,
Made and re-made, redeemed to rediscover
Worth as inestimable
As the deep night sky.

(July 2019, Lee Abbey)

Jo Heydon

Jo Heydon lives in Rock, North Cornwall with her husband Roger and many goldfish. A former editor, copywriter and crossword compiler she writes now for her own amusement – and hopefully for others.

Bliss

You're away!
What bliss.
I can do
What I like
How I like
When I like.

But there's
A space
A hush
A chill
And then you're back!
What bliss.

Love 1

Twenty minutes after their return from the hospital he broke the silence.
“Well, I now know, exactly what I am facing.”
“What WE are facing, my darling, I will be with you all the way”.
“Oh! A cliché; I expect we’ll have a great many more of those before I die. Speaking of which…” he reached from the wheelchair with difficulty and caught her arm, “I don’t intend that this should be a long, drawn-out affair, but I will need your help. I’m sure you and I understand each other on that.”
“I can’t.” she said
“You would if you loved me.”
“IF! IF I loved you? You know I do. But do you love ME? Because, if you do, don’t ask.”
“So now I don’t love you because I ask the only thing of you which you can give me now.”
“I don’t think I could bear to, besides…”
“Besides what? The law? The law’s an ass. Is it better to watch me suffer or help me?”
“It’s not that simple – and in any case we don’t have to face it yet.”
“Oh but we do, my darling, we do; and there is this. I would do it for you. Because I adore you.”
“That is unfair of you,” she said, and turned away.
“Don’t make me beg,” he said, “allow me a little dignity.”
“Will you STOP! Just stop. I don’t know how or what I can do but yes, I will help because I love you that much. But not yet.”
“Thank you. No, not yet – and I will tell you how. But it must be before I lose my speech. I want my last words to be for you, and the last voice I hear to be yours. My love.”

Love 2

Oh wow! Babe! You're back! LOVE the tan. How was it? No! Let's see. O.M.G! It's gorgeous – must be at least one carat. I am soooo jealous.
Love the shoes, by the way – where d'you get them? Figures. I love the way the Italians do shoes.
Me? Well – same old, same old, still working with the old people. "my old ducks" I call them. Love 'em to bits really. But never mind that – I've met someone special. Course; or I wouldn't be telling you would I? He's well fit, if you catch my drift and I love the way he dresses – sort of quirky but smartish. Hard to describe. We met at this gig – Arianne Grande – yes – really! Don't you love her – she's so brave – yeah.
Anyway, got back to his, sunk a bottle of prosecco – he's quite sophisticated I suppose. Early days but I might be in love – honestly!

So go on then, back to you Babes – what am I going to wear? As your bridesmaid you muppet. You promised, remember? Anything but yellow. Or cream or that sort of sludgy pink. What do you mean I'm not? We're best friends! I thought you loved me!
You selfish pig. Love? You don't know the meaning of the word.

Jo Higson

Jo Higson lives on the Barbican, Plymouth and is currently undertaking an MA in Creative Writing at the University of Plymouth. She works in the voluntary sector and is a life coach, having had careers in archaeology, the civil service and as a birth doula.

Love: The End

My heart broke as I was driving along the Atlantic Highway. I was on my way to a work conference taking place in a beautiful lakeside venue. Until that moment I had clearly been in denial, in shock. My heart had felt huge, red and raw: painful but intact.

A familiar song came on the radio – a song I had enjoyed many times for its haunting melody and the aching beauty of the velvet male voice. Never before had the words held significance: in the past I had sung along almost mechanically. But this time they struck like a well-aimed, finely sharpened steel arrow, piercing my heart. In a beat my heart cracked and then shattered. No longer sore, bruised and swollen, it fractured into sharp edges, painfully cutting my very being. I had to stop the car in a lay-by close to my destination as the pain was unbearable. I clutched the steering wheel and sobbed and sobbed as the pain engulfed me.

But I had to go on. I had to be there and I had to be an active participant. I swept up the broken pieces and deposited them back where my heart was meant to be, dried my eyes, stilled my ragged breaths and drove on to present a façade of the person I used to be.

Now, two, no three, years later my heart is once again intact, pink, beating steadily and regularly with the only signs of damage, a few tender darker bruised patches that on occasion I probe to see if the pain has finally gone.

(May 2019)

Helen Jagger

Helen Jagger's poems have been published in the UK, US and Australia. She runs The Poetry Society's North Cornwall Stanza, many poetry workshops and has facilitated the Indian King Poets. She was poet in residence at Pencarrow from 2010 –2012, and in 2014 she worked with the Falmouth Poetry Group on a new poetry festival.

Jessica's Confession

From "Living by the Risks of Love", a liturgy based on Shakespeare's *The Merchant of Venice*

My mother married for love but when she died,
did she want *me* to stay with *father*, his unpaid
unthanked maid?

He orders me, advises me to lock
the doors, to barricade myself against
the wars outside

as if the light and air themselves abuse us
when it's our empty home that hurts us most,
that smells of death.

One love may hide another love. The first?
Correct and decent, filial. The second,
boundless as the sea.

The second love feels right. A wild love,
tidal-strong and fierce, confuses me,
but is it wrong

To go or not to go? Pulled two ways,
my body tears. My heart's held by Lorenzo,
but my duty's here.

A FESTIVAL OF LOVE

My father's anger at the world, his grief,
abrade my soul as if my flesh was flayed,
all nerves exposed.

I'll not be swallowed by my father's need!
My duty's like tight chain, but love can cut it.
I'll open the shutters

as I have my eyes, unbolt the doors.
If I stay, I'll be a creature of the dark:
I'll go with Lorenzo.

I'll be his wife and loyal to him,
as Leah to you, Father. I am too full
of love to stay.

John May

John May lives in Tiverton, Devon. He is a gifted writer, artist, musician and craftsman. He was rector and prebendary of the Collegiate Church of St Endellion from 2007 to 2014.

fragment

Sometimes I wonder if love is like this, –
        a passion for beauty
                on a hot, drifting day,
dreaming laughter in the hot, hot place,
        warm air making away
                with cool corners, a flirtation
        lying between life's naked sheets
                in a room of
        oak furniture and blue china,
offering one's senses to the world,
        a cosmic flirtation,
and her, or her, or tomorrow her,
        in particular.

At other times I reflect upon Wittgenstein.

(When teaching in Dordogne College, Mussidan, France, 1979-80)

A love song for my wife and my Christ,
whose birthdays are at the end of the year, and both of whom speak Old English and Spanish.
Feliz cumpleaños = Happy Birthday!

The days are spun to the yeares end
and you are fair beyond;
so too my love doth weave and wend
its way to you with song,
Ah! Feliz cumpleaños.

The years are mickle swift and fleet
and you are fair beyond;
eache day with you so dear and sweet
as jasmine in the winter alle so long,
Ah! Feliz cumpleaños.

O fair one come away with me
for you are fair beyond;
¡Oye! Dance, sing, laugh and spree
the bells themselves will ring ding-dong,
Ah! Feliz cumpleaños.

Ah! Sweetling born at the yeares end,
and you are fair beyond;
this late December day my love to you I send
and e'er and ay will say my whole life long
Ah! Feliz cumpleaños.

The lost keys of Love & Wisdom

This is the unlockable under the stormclouds
with the wild wind tearing at the gate over the moor
when I come home and have forgotten the key,
forgotten the key,
when I come home and her heart is shut tight,
and I stumble and pull the shroud of despair over my wild eyes
and in the darkness fall and fall
under the weight
of hopes now beaten back by disappointments;
just so the blotched autumn leaves skelter
through skies, brush against my face and die in
spinning futility in dark treacherous corners
outside her door.

All my life I also sought the key and way to wisdom:
I stayed up all night, talked until dawn,
walked barefoot to Skye,
sat on mountaintops in the mist and rain,
sang chants and studied metaphysics,
always seeking the gateway beyond.

At the gates of Wisdom and Love
the searchers root through their pockets
for the key, the code, the way, the
thought they left behind,
all fumble in volumes,
all ransack bags of papers,
all rake desperate hands through their long romantic
scenarios,
look at their feet, peer into the distance, despair
outside her door.

A FESTIVAL OF LOVE

There was an insect who half flew,
half blundered, flopped and dragged
his multitude of legs and spindly awkward bits
through the keyhole
and came out in the provinces of Love and Wisdom.
But it was very dull
and he went home again.
He much preferred the struggle,
the flopping and blundering,
the curious half flight, the pain and ecstasy,
and, above all, the constant restless search.

(15:i:19)

Judith Pollinger

Judith Pollinger lives in the parish of St Endellion. She is a retired priest who continues to minister in North Cornwall. She has always loved poetry and is a member of the St Endellion Poetry Group.

Last Dance

(For Lauren)

Part girl, part woman now;
still part of me
though we were parted long ago
and I was left grieving.

Does she recall that time
when trustingly, her hand in mine,
we skipped through Autumn leaves
on that last day?

Now, I bring to you
that dancing two year old;
you with the wounded hands
and wounded side.

I bring her bright face
her laughing eyes
and place her hand in yours;
help me to let go.

Laying Out

Once, when someone died
they'd send for a woman
practised in the art of laying out.

These days a nurse will come,
or, undertaker's men—
except, that when you died
and we, your child and mine
stood lost beside the bed,
the nurse asked, 'Would you like to help?'

We fetched a bowl, warm water, soap
and towel, washed your cooling flesh,
exclaimed how thin you were.

We dressed you in fresh clothes
and combed your hair,
but jibbed at shaving you;
glad, more glad than we could say,
to do for you these last small acts of love.

Estelle Price

Estelle Price completed an MA in Creative Writing at the University of Manchester in 2016. She is the winner of the 2018 Book *of Kells Writing Competition and her poetry has been placed or short-listed in Canterbury Poet of the Year.*

The voyage
(for John and Emily)

and after a joy-lit night of dancing,
when love must leave the chateau,
we'll give them a canoe to drift downriver.
he'll lift her delicate bones and ivory silk,
settle his bride in the wide arc of his heart,
as her small hands paddle the opening
bars of their wedded-song.

grape-scented days, where laughter ripens
the vines, time tangles in the reeds.

and when love finds the sea
we'll give them a dingy with tanbark sails
and an anchor it takes two to lift.
scudding across the Atlantic, hands knotted
on the helm, she'll smooth the chart
under a shy moon plump with promises,
one tack after another into the wind.

salted-days, where touch is the only
currency and time leaps with dolphins.

and should love grow tired
of shifting tides, we'll give them
a narrowboat with fore and aft decks
and room for a basket of purple olives.
moored beside a mulberry tree,
pup asleep on her knee, they'll rock
their life-ship over the ripples.

birdsong-days, where time dissolves
in the river and marriage finds its melody.

Blind date

Love met us at the pleasure gardens – delicate
in her holiday best – uncertain if she should stay.

Beside a bed of daisies (waiting to be chained)
we walked the three of us: her in-between. Too soon

to reach across her breasts to find each other's secret
door we sat, chipped statues, two ends of a bench

half in shadow half in sun. I cannot now remember
what was said except you asked if I was cold

and I replied *not at all* for Love had crept inside
my shoe to tingle silver needles on my sole.

Crushing the shingle

There we were bundled on Aldeburgh beach,
my winter coat flapping in the east wind unable
to shield the new life that simmered, your generous
smile at risk of being snatched by a jealous

gull and flown over the North Sea. We knew
nothing then. Believed each rounded stone
a blessing waiting to be claimed as we sat
on a memorial bench and fed fish and chips

into each other's mouths beside the derelict
lookout. Through all the years since of turning
tides and sandbanks, our ghosts have drowsed,
waiting to be woken in the peeling beachside

pavilion. Now, in Aldeburgh again, as each boot
crushes the shingle, my hand fits into the pocket
of another and I hear a sigh as the past sets
hard as if two ants are tangled in amber fossil.

Christopher Southgate

Christopher Southgate is a theologian, scientist and poet who teaches in the University of Exeter. As well as theological books on the questions of suffering and evil in the universe, he has published eight volumes of poetry and has been commended in the National Poetry Competition.

Portia

From "Living by the Risks of Love", a liturgy based on Shakespeare's *The Merchant of Venice*

She was always too tall, too blonde,
She stood out, talked too much,
Eyes flashing, scared boys.
                        In she walked, alarmingly,
In each ear, hoops of purest gold.
Down each wrist, shaken bangles of silver.
Through her pierced navel, a leaden ring.

Then it was known she was plenty rich enough
But entangled, hemmed in by conditions
None had dared try to meet.
                        This she told, tantalisingly,
In each ear, hoops of purest gold.
Down each wrist, shaken bangles of silver.
Through her pierced navel, a leaden ring.

To try to force her winning gallery
Meant unbearable hazard, risk
Of never playing the game again.
                        So she still lived, longingly,

In each ear, hoops of purest gold.
Down each wrist, shaken bangles of silver.
Through her pierced navel, a leaden ring.

Three, eventually, had a cut at the test
(Her own heart in hiding)
Until she was seen, at last, for herself.
                    Then, at last, she danced,
In each ear, hoops of purest gold.
Down each wrist, shaken bangles of silver.
Through her pierced navel, a leaden ring.

At court she fitted in, finally, playing a part.
Ringlets pinned inside a lawyer's cap,
Plain cross of filigreed silver
Stern against a tunic of sable,
Pierced navel now reserved
For the reverence of her new lover.
Through it, worn with joy,
                    A leaden ring.

David Steven

David Steven is a retired priest living in Wadebridge, Cornwall. He has written poetry all his life.

The Mary Magdalene Frontal in the Morning Chapel, Lincoln Cathedral

Only the tumbling hair, bright jewelled
shines against the black material
of a Laudian Front. And near the floor
an equal jewelled jar to make a ferial
day festive with sacrificial love. More
is unknown, save maybe that encounter
with a gardener, straw-hatted in some art,
equally distributed by her or us.
Only the hair and the unbroken jar apart
recall us to our own unbroken heart.

In a seaside café at Gorran Haven

I’m still surprised how much they have to say,
husbands and wives, each in their own way,
at the seaside café table day after day.
I would have expected it to be more so at night
when lovers must confirm by hearing and by sight
that each is much more likely to be right.
After long years, you’d think they’d know by now
and in some silence reaffirm their vow.

Child and Mother – Treliske Hospital

There is a moment to walk hand in hand,
a mother and her son who can stand
quite unselfconscious of the cord or strand
of love that holds them still together.

Later another will hold his hand in hers,
still both oblivious how the world observes
lovers and laughter, enfleshed hopes and fears
of love that holds them both together.

Small hands clasp fingers until size
allows them freedom to be separated and eyes
alone can hope a daughter's wise
in the exchange of hands you've made together.

A moment comes when the first hand is all
that dying memories can retrieve, recall,
and son and mother in a moment's thrall
enact the contact they once had together.

Mrs Arnolfini Replies to her Husband. Van Eyck 1434

This is a serious moment in their lives
so grave looks are in order for Van Eyck,
and both Arnolfinis have to strive
to hold a hand, resist a smile
or ask, "Why did you leave that apple
on the sill, my dear?" "Ah sir,
perfection is a doubtful game in love;
your sombre gown fur trimmed
and that enormous hat I told you not to wear.
My sumptuous bed and crimson hangings,
my best green dress with my expectant child
all speak of our prosperity in life. But love
is not so tidy everywhere; it scatters round the rooms
of all our lives the unexpected and the trite,
enough to say, "wealth and perfection may not last
and some untidiness recalls, even for us,
in this grand room, that love has normal moments;"
two pairs of shoes left lying, as to say,
"This is a home, things happen, get left out,
and you who love order and control
have lost it here." In the small mirror
Between them both, the artist is witness
to a less tidy love that is complete,
her seriousness made just more human
by the small dog at their feet.

Jenny Swan

Jenny Swan lives on the North Coast of Cornwall. She has recently published a book. She is a member of the St Endellion Poetry Group.

First Day – Last Day

On the first day that we met
and spoke about
inconsequential things;
the weather, the journey
and our feelings for both.
How we would keep in touch
always stay friends
even if things went wrong,
no pressure, just friends.
For ever.

Our love affair was passionate;
nearly everyone disapproved.
But it didn't bother us.
We had each other,
and always would.

On that last day we met
and spoke about
inconsequential things;
the weather, the journey
and our feelings for both.
How we would keep in touch.
Always stay friends.

No pressure.
Just friends.

Your Hand

I can feel your hand on my back
just resting there.
And I know it is you.
I know you are here.

Can you feel my hand on your back
just resting there.
Does it feel like me?
Do you know I am here.

Did you feel it
resting there.
Intimate somehow.
Special and somehow meaningful.

I felt your hand on my back;
Special and intimate.
A memory to be treasured.
A feeling yearned for again.

Felicity Tattersall

Felicity Tattersall lives in Falmouth and is a writer and illustrator (Children's books and short stories). She is inspired by archives, museums and history.

Follow your own path. The others don't lead anywhere (Self-Love Mantra)

Allured by the clarity gold at the centre of the labyrinthine maze, I started walking, saw footprints so I knew I must be right, because someone else had been there before me. The melodic familiarity of those footsteps, led me. Proxy, passive, not looking around me, slipping into my own reverie. Until the footsteps stopped, cliff edge. I was left desperately alone. I groped forward, wearier than a sloth, and smacked the crown of my head onto the overhanging dead end. Despondent my ears overflowed with laughter. Pulse quickened. I chased that laughter, intrigued, becoming ever more the pursuer. I wanted to live inside that laughter. It was behind every leaf and shadow. The harder I chased it, the fainter it seemed to become. It out-ran me. A milk like comfort path opened up. Gossamer soft, apricot low lit. I got stuck in that honeyed loveliness, and made no progress for about ten years, nearly forgetting all about the gold. Until finally, I was so overwhelmed by the mindless gorgeousness. A memory stone smacks me, reminding me to seek that centre. Delicious wafts draw me onto another path. My nose sated, but my other senses left frustrated. The path fizzled out. Utter despair enveloped me. There were no more paths to follow. I looked down. I looked up. I looked everywhere. Until I 'felt' through. The maze. Was just a PROJECTION. All that time. Beneath it was the most terrible and fearsome path of all. On that path I could only see myself, only answer to myself, only follow and lead myself. This path was strangely barren, unstrewn of distractions, and all of a sudden I knew bald, bare and broken as it was, it was beautiful and would lead me wherever I wanted to go.

Chris Woods

Chris Woods, a GP for many years, is now semi-retired and lives in Holcombe Village near Ramsbottom with his wife Brenda. They are spending increasingly more time at their place in Trelights, North Cornwall. Chris has had two collections of poetry published, ***Recovery*** *(Enitharmon) and* ***Dangerous Driving*** *(Comma Press).*

Katy

Six months old

Wakes us at dawn
with a soprano chorus

Dances on her back
to music we cannot hear

Conducts the orchestra
with a hand or rattle

Smiles, as she bends
her body into a grin

Puts fists in her mouth
to make her tongue talk

Opens her arms to us
and our hearts to her

Fastens a wet medal
of saliva to my shirt

Curls tongue and toes
as she takes her bottle

A FESTIVAL OF LOVE

Kicks against my chest
like my heart beating

Watches her mobiles
and parents go round

Stares out into space
as worlds we cannot see

Shows us how we were
light years distant

Lifts hands above head
and surrenders to sleep

Scaffolding

A steel cocoon
envelops their flat.
The outlook changes.
Ideas take shape.

She sees blueprints
in the lines of steel.
She becomes
an architect of change.

He sees the structure
falling apart.
The pieces depend
too much on each other.

She sees the parts
joining together,
as relationships
are built in steel.

He sees the bars
outside their window.
He feels confined
and wants to escape.

She sees a nest
and then cats-cradles,
now climbing frames
for her children.

Cocooned in her arms,
his outlook changes.
Ideas take shape
as steel hugs brick.

47438130R00036

Printed in Poland
by Amazon Fulfillment
Poland Sp. z o.o., Wrocław